BRAIN POPS
Cryptograms

Published by Adams Media, an F+W Publications Company
57 Littlefield Street
Avon, MA 02322
www.adamsmedia.com

ISBN: 1-59337-559-X

Printed in Canada

J I H G F E D C B A

This publication is designed to provide accurate and authoritative infor-
mation with regard to the subject matter covered. It is sold with the
understanding that the publisher is not engaged in rendering legal,
accounting, or other professional advice. If legal advice or other expert
assistance is required, the services of a competent professional person
should be sought.
—From a *Declaration of Principles* jointly adopted by a
Committee of the American Bar Association and
a Committee of Publishers and Associations

The content in this book was provided by Nikki Katz.

GETTING STARTED

In this book, the puzzles use simple substitutions to encrypt the quotations that you'll try to solve. Each letter will be replaced by a different letter but the original spacing and punctuation will remain in place. Since you will not be given the key, your job is to decipher the puzzle using the topic given and your knowledge of the English language.

Common Letters and Words

In English, E is the most common letter, followed by T, A, and O, and N, I, and R. The words A and I are the most common one-letter words, with O coming in at a very distant third place. The most common two-letter words are OF, TO, IN, IS, IT, BE, BY, HE, AS, ON, AT, OR, AN, SO, IF, and NO. The most common three-letter words are THE and AND, followed by FOR, HIS, NOT, BUT, YOU, ARE, HER, and HAD. The most common four-letter word is THAT, followed by WITH, HAVE, and FROM. If you see a four-letter word that begins and ends in the same letter, you might want to try "that" first.

The letter Q is always followed by U. E is the most common letter at the end of a word. T is the most common letter at the beginning of a word. If there is an apostrophe in the puzzle, it means that the word is either possessive (John's) or it is a contraction (won't). If a single letter follows the apostrophe, it's usually an S or a T. If the letter is a T, the letter before the apostrophe is an N.

Don't Forget the Vowels

When it comes to vowels, the majority of two-letter words start with an A, I, O, or U and end with an E, O, or Y. The letters O and E are often seen in double letters, whereas the other vowels are rarely seen. The letter A is usually seen as the initial letter in a word or the second letter from the end. The letter E is usually seen as the second letter in a word or the final letter, but is also scattered throughout words. The letter I is most often seen as the third letter from the end (ION and ING being common endings). The letter O is usually seen as the second letter in a word or the final letter. The letter U is typically seen as the first letter in a word or the second letter from the end. The letter Y is usually the last letter in a word.

Where Do I Start?

Solving cryptograms involves a lot of trial and error. You may want to start out by counting the letters and guessing that the most common letter is an E. Although this often gives you a good jump-start, there may be a few puzzles that have no Es at all. Knowing one or two letters of a word can often help you solve the rest of the word and gives you letters in other words within the puzzle. Words that commonly go together, like "it is" can be helpful as well. Longer cryptograms are easier to solve than shorter ones because they offer more instances of letters and patterns for you to view.

Bookworm Cryptograms

Homer 1

Z WGTGMT TPOT QOU FPN PZWGM NUG TPZUV ZU TPG WGCTPM NJ PZM PGOKT, OUW MCGORM JNK OUNTPGK.

Homer 2

WV WZ EKSJAAN FLLEDZWGE VF ZCEEM J HSEZV ORF OFSAM AWXE VF ZVJN JDM VF MEVJWD FDE ORF WZ JDPWFSZ VF AEJGE.

Edgar Allan Poe 1

Z AFRBI IJYZHJ, ZH WNZJY, DGJ EFJDNO FY AFNIM KM DGJ NGODGXZSKB SNJKDZFH FY WJKRDO. ZDM MFBJ KNWZDJN ZM DKMDJ.

Edgar Allan Poe 2

WB, FACJASDJPZ A NERERLEN AJ IWC AS JBE LPEWM FEDERLEN;
WSF EWDB CEYWNWJE FZASX ERLEN INKQXBJ AJC XBKCJ QYKS JBE GPKKN.

William Shakespeare 1

WHIDD E GZKNITM VHMM VZ I WPKKMT'W RIF? VHZP ITV
KZTM DZUMDF ILR KZTM VMKNMTIVM: TZPYH XELRW RZ
WHIAM VHM RITDELY BPRW ZQ KIF, ILR WPKKMT'W DMIWM
HIVH IDD VZZ WHZTV I RIVM.

William Shakespeare 2

MC RSX NOZNFK SO DZCNXRCAA. ASHC NZC MSZR DZCNX,
ASHC NGQFCUC DZCNXRCAA, NRK ASHC QNUC DZCNXRCAA
XQZVAX VWSR 'CH.

Henry David Thoreau 1

TOQ CPJ VOG IGQA PWGJQ ZPJ ATPUT TGRPH, LYT OQ VOG
TUPDQWA VXTO PJGTOQU CYAT VPXT TXWW TOPT GTOQU
XA UQPRH.

Henry David Thoreau 2

EGB WXKE C MFS OX TXA WN TACBSO CK KCWVZN EX YB
GCK TACBSO. C GFDB SX QBFZEG EX YBKEXQ XS GCW. CT
GB HSXQK EGFE C FW GFVVN CS ZXDCSR GCW, GB QCZZ
QFSE SX XEGBA ABQFAO. CK SXE TACBSOKGCV OCDCSB
CS EGCK?

J. R. R. Tolkien 1

N FAGUNHOOX UNPONLT HOOTCAGX NS HOO NKP
YHSNRTPKHHKNASP, HSU HOJHXP IHMT UAST PNSFT N CGTJ
AOU HSU JHGX TSAWCI KA UTKTFK NKP EGTPTSFT.

J. R. R. Tolkien 2

I ZJX LYTAJVT AYHCRD, ORW, JU PYF, WRT CJPFRH
TURIDVUR YHDYFR YD AYF.

Mark Twain 1

OZSSROY JRZ MYUY IX TDTRA . . . IXD OZSSROY JRZ MYUY
I WYWFYU RC QRXGUYOO . . . FZA T UYSYIA WJOYVC.

Mark Twain 2

BQS FNJO KUO BF XSSP OFGZ QSUJBQ DC BF SUB KQUB
OFG RFN'B KUNB, RZDNX KQUB OFG RFN'B JDXS, UNR RF
KQUB OFG'R ZUBQSZ NFB.

Other Authors 1

HQK IUK CKEB JQ SUDDB XSQK MSQB RC KCM UWWOHQ
MSUM MSQ CJGQIM CT EYTQ YW SUDDYKQWW.
— ZQCNZQ CNXQEE

Other Authors 2

OPKE JLKGGT SHYRSN AL YBE IN K WYYS EPKE, OPLH TYB'JL
KGG DYHL JLKDIHZ IE, TYB OINP EPL KBEPYJ EPKE OJYEL IE
OKN K ELJJIVIR VJILHD YV TYBJN KHD TYB RYBGD RKGG
PIA BX YH EPL XPYHL OPLHLCLJ TYB VLGE GISL IE.
—U. D. NKGIHZLJ

Other Authors 3

LQQRCVYLIYSP YU L KSPFCRBOH IWYPM: YI ALGCU KWLI
YU CJVCHHCPI YP SIWCRU NCHSPM IS OU LU KCHH.
—ZSHILYRC

9

Other Authors 4

H WXQWSA XHLN RO LMOQ NKNTSRDHMJ WUOBR ZS MNQ
FTHNMPA, WMP MORDHMJ WUOBR ZS OXP OMNA.

—OAVWT QHXPN

Other Authors 5

JBDBZ VZFGV TJAVLOJE VLTV QTJ VLOJC WPZ OVGBYW OW
APF QTJ'V GBB MLBZB OV CBBSG OVG NZTOJ.

—K. C. ZPMYOJE

Other Authors 6

SMXDX IG KVAT MGCDI MVFX JXXA IHXAZ BA NGAFBANBAP
KTIXRO ZMVZ B VK DBPMZ, BI ZMXDX AGZ IGKX DXVIGA ZG
OXVD B KVT JX SDGAP?   —EVAX VCIZXA

Other Authors 7

MC SJD PJX'H GEBL HGL HMIL HJ ZLEP, SJD PJX'H GEBL
HGL HMIL JZ HGL HJJWF HJ QZMHL.   —FHLKGLX AMXN

Other Authors 8

SG LXH OHA IVG IFZ NIO LXIK OHA QGGW, SGUIANG KXHNG LXH CEFZ ZHF'K CIKKGV IFZ KXHNG LXH CIKKGV ZHF'K CEFZ. —ZV. NGANN

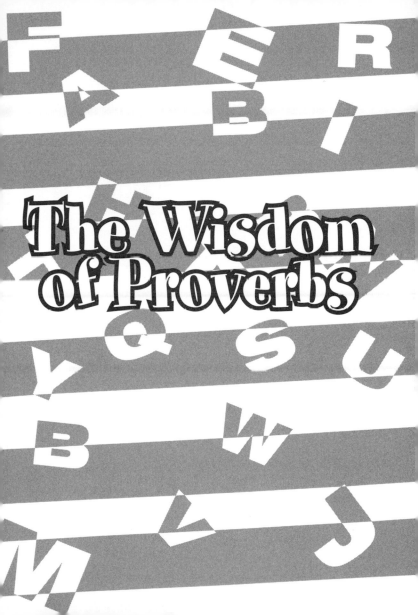

The Wisdom of Proverbs

American Proverbs 1
BCJ CSFJN CPPE BEFSYJ XMJR SZ SN RP TPRCJV BKTJ ZP
CSFJ B KBE JABQUTJ.

American Proverbs 2
UZS CVB CYR LCYK ICTB LFQHB AZG OCA, YZ OZSYQYV IGY
HCIKI C LFZHB RCA.

American Proverbs 3
M RKIP KT MRBPDIFAC FI KTAPO MI OPPRTNJ MI M RKIP KT
XPRFYFOP.

American Proverbs 4
JNA KEBA CBGOKAQJU IEO YDQ, JNA RAYAB RBDAQHU IEO
YDFF NCZA.

American Proverbs 5
MGQY W UYFSY, SJWPWSZYP SWFFCZ RY HZPYFKZJYFYD
RI EJGZYEWHJ.

14

American Proverbs 6

C RJUJFWGJUZ OCU LIWEGY CGGWM C NJM NCEGZL HU
IHOLJGN ZW BJJA IHL NSHJUYL HU KWEUZJUCUKJ.

American Proverbs 7

FT FG HYL MOID TS JYMM SOT SJ Y TBFKTXXVTB-GTSKZ
NFVLSN SV JKFLYZ.

American Proverbs 8

QLLK FHXW LFLA OCTL HKLD NLRHWL VIWWCIGL, YIJR
AYXM IRMLWOIWTA.

Chinese Proverbs 1

IJNF E KEA E UJYQ EAH VBW UFFH QJK UBM E HEV. PFERQ E
KEA PB UJYQ EAH VBW UFFH QJK UBM E DJUFPJKF.

Chinese Proverbs 2

KR WKQ ALNL YL A XQQS XQG XYHR ZYJMORL, EMO KR
WKQ BQRL JQO ALN GRZAYJL A XQQS XQGRHRG.

Chinese Proverbs 3

KSPT URZ SYOP RTBU LKR CPTTNPW BPHL NT LSP KRFBX, DZU Y BRYH RH DFPYX KNLS RTP, YTX Y BNBU KNLS LSP RLSPF.

Chinese Proverbs 4

QRZ GAUMK QRZ SRLG QRZD ARDLV? IAR KMRIL, AV HWQ FDUMX W IARSV AVDO FWYK GR QRZ LRHVOWQ.

Chinese Proverbs 5

J QUESRZ EN NGHSGRS BWG ZJRPSN BELW XGF ER LWS NFRIETWL JRZ BJIMN KSNEZS XGF ER LWS NWJZGBN.

Chinese Proverbs 6

GORH VMS JPR FMMP, HRUKOCMPW TEMWR CV GUEE HMZ TMYR; MHTR VMS CRTMYR PUTO, VMS'EE CR WSPFPUWRB CV NUWUZW DPMY (JEERKRB) PREJZUNRW JDJP.

Chinese Proverbs 7

R EHHF NHCLDGV ZRS NHCMHFV R MRF XDBP, QKWBK ZRS WG LDCG FWOEDWOV R EHHF NHCLDGV.

Chinese Proverbs 8

LNDDRBPZZ RZ TRVP N ZFBAPNU, ELRHL CLP TPNZC
ZLNJWE RBCPQHPDCZ, ELRTP NJSPQZRCG RZ WMCPB NZ
CLP QNRB WM ZDQRBY.

English Proverbs 1

QLD'O XLGDO RLGE XUCXZVDI BVKLEV OUVR'EV UYOXUVQ.

English Proverbs 2

R IKDQ KF BAU ARFQ KC XMDBA RXM KF BAU INCA.

English Proverbs 3

XOP FJARR LR ABSAGR FJPPTPJ KT XOP KXOPJ RLWP KD
XOP DPTEP.

English Proverbs 4

C PHHV IZWPRHD ACI CD RCPTR'I RMR, C TQHD'I ARCWO,
CDV C TCVM'I ACDV.

English Proverbs 5

QICMS AW YQZ IXZ QICMS AW CPGQ LIBQG I LIX OQIMAOS,
JQIMAOS, IXZ JPGQ.

English Proverbs 6

Q HQE HQC JXQA Q NSBGX TS LQTXB, MZT PQEEST HQIX
NKH ABKEI.

English Proverbs 7

QG KQOK GOKJ CS KQG FTPM'J MCCJG JQOVV IG NQCFGW
HTKQ SGOKQGAJ.

English Proverbs 8

VRJDJ ZH FGVRZFX BRZER BJ DJEJZMJ BZVR HG TNER
DJSNEVOFEJ OH OKMZEJ.

French Proverbs 1

OKRYHIG BD F SKLFI; BO MKH IGNUGCY ZGR YKTFM TK IKY
GEVGCY YK RGNFBI ZGR YKLKRRKS.

French Proverbs 2

LNRJ! QY KJRP, RQZ DYW RPV BYIQB YWJ JY KVR? ORPENIQB,
RQZ DYW NRSV QY OWKIE? JPRSVAIQB, RQZ DYW NRSV QY
CYYT? LNRJ! QY AYSV, RQZ DYW RPV BYIQB YWJ JY AISV?

French Proverbs 3

J CAV QZJMVCU ZYHKB QLV DYZCB DLACV QZHQL AU
NHQQAKW LVZ SYYQU YK.

French Proverbs 4

CAG SKKY XOE NKXXOEFI YGISGNC; CAG ZGLLOY XVIC
OMTOBI GDNWCG OELGY.

French Proverbs 5

LDCVMULUZIS LO M YLDI JB PSMYDSOO; NXSESV QSD MVS
DJU ZDCVMUSBZX.

French Proverbs 6

WH DZC GOUDOL UPLCR DZC RPX RCCR WD, KPD WH ZC
JWBBR DZC CFLDZ ZWGCR WD.

French Proverbs 7
MU MZ QVHO SU UFD UEDD HQSLDL TMUF IERMU UFSU
UFD CDQCHD UFEQT ZUQVDZ.

French Proverbs 8
ZJHT OK IMT UDRP JQ YDCCODAT, DPU YDCCODAT OK IMT
KVPKTI JQ ZJHT.

Italian Proverbs 1
BHDD KUB VDD JUN FKUZ, EHDGHLH KUB VDD JUN XHVR,
SU KUB VDD JUN VRH VEDH.

Italian Proverbs 2
FN PJX VDPFXIP BFXE, PJX BWGPWC JDE QFAAXB JFY, HUP
FN JX MXPE TXAA, PJX EDFIPE JDLX EDLXB JFY.

Italian Proverbs 3
SAOU JUADHUW RMPJCUY JMW CTYD DAYY LMP TWU
TCVUI ZMW AD.

Italian Proverbs 4

VKJTKKW HCPNWG CWD DSNWG BCWP C LCNO SZ HQSKH NH
TSOW SYJ.

Italian Proverbs 5

KU ZQFKUT O RMJXL OUP HOYKUT O DKBL, XRQH FMQJ
LFLX OUP WMIILUP FMQJXLSB HM TMP.

Italian Proverbs 6

NQTT GKBY HTFLL JPWZ QR QL WSARG, WSARG QR JPWZ
QR QL NBTT, ZWVWY TWFVW QR WSARG, ZWVWY TWFVW
QR NBTT.

Italian Proverbs 7

B MSDWZJY DZBD GPJI DP DZJ AJQQ PHDJT SI QSRJQX DP
GJD KYPRJT.

Italian Proverbs 8

FEHKH VX WB WHHO FB YVWO ZC BWH'X EHIO YHJBKH VF
VX YKBDHW.

Japanese Proverbs 1
NH LKQ OWXJY QV ANIP X JXNA LKQ BNAA GPW SXMMPUPY YKBJ.

Japanese Proverbs 2
QMDMGL CMSXGYS BESMGL MD OBPOHVBR. BESMGL CMSXGYS QMDMGL MD LMZXSRBHV.

Japanese Proverbs 3
X KRCTOE XYYAF RK EXKROV LYAUEC, LJW CAW WEC RC X LJCDOE.

Japanese Proverbs 4
KBJJBU JV KB X EUZGJXP XOH JV KB KUVRBO, JAXO JV KB X JMPB NTVO JAB AVNGBJVT.

Japanese Proverbs 5
TIM'W NJRIHBJ IVJN CHA WCPW UIJQ, ZJXINJ LIG QJJ CHA WCPW BIAJQ.

Japanese Proverbs 6
UQ U XBHHMB AVMS, US RVUJA; UQ U XBHHMB QMLGR,
SEB IUJH NMLIA.

Japanese Proverbs 7
SI GZY JSWE HZ RNTLP HEN ESCENWH HLYHEW, ONCSP
JSHE HEN TRQETONH.

Japanese Proverbs 8
VAZAQ WQPNW I LXDIV, AZAV RF N.IA .IIN OXQVA CXP NAZAV
BJRMTQAV.

Native American Proverbs 1
EA EW LIAAIG AV QJMI TIWW AQYHRIG EH AQI FVYAQ JHR
FVGI TESQAHEHS EH AQI QJHR.

Native American Proverbs 2
RISAR RLS SAIRL PSBB. WR PAO DMR NWXSD RM YMH
JY YMHI QAISDRO, WR PAO BMADSU RM YMH JY YMHI
GLWBUISD.

Native American Proverbs 3

MA PAE QOMHK BAOL PKVHWNAL OPEVF BAO YRFJ EYA
GAAPT VP WVT GAZZRTVPT.

Native American Proverbs 4

GVW DNB'Z TNYF N MFHXVB TEV LX MHFZFBJLBI ZV CF
NXOFFM.

Native American Proverbs 5

K SBZSYB PALRZOL RANLZFQ AN YAGB PAXU ZX LRB
IOMMKYZ HFKNN.

Native American Proverbs 6

UTCYR SXWSO DP OWFDMDSQ SN YMM TCNTMC. NPMQ
SOCP GYP QNW AC Y SXWC FYP.

Native American Proverbs 7

CQO'U VHAW YBPDOC TB; D THX OQU ABHC. CQO'U VHAW
DO NSQOU QN TB; D THX OQU NQAAQV. VHAW YBEDCB TB
UPHU VB THX YB HE QOB.

Native American Proverbs 8
U JUE OUE'N MFN YPOA PG AF NUQFH XYIXFY OUYF IG APH
GUJPZK.

Spanish Proverbs 1
AM SNJ FYWR KN W LNNZ KUYY SNJ EAFF BY DUNKYOKYZ
BS W LNNZ PHWZNE.

Spanish Proverbs 2
WO XHKD EWOB EVGCY CH CADHE XHK HOO CAR DHHO,
CDX CH OWGR V ZHE HGB.

Spanish Proverbs 3
TNDD FN UBG CJ WK KGIE JCRN XSR C'DD TNDD KGI UBG
KGI XEN.

Spanish Proverbs 4
YME'G HFQKW IEOQHH DMI AKE JRFZMSQ IFME GCQ
HJOQEAQ.

Spanish Proverbs 5
OPXU, DIGN, INJ FPNUH YINNPV TU SUDV MUYEUV; VCUH
MPPN TUVEIH VCUFMUOXUM.

Spanish Proverbs 6
GM NJMZO NR XYNNT CH SNAEL BNAO ELGM G DNJMT NR
RACOMTHLCD.

Spanish Proverbs 7
B GBC KPL VXHUSA PHGASFT LC PHA BCQSAZXO HA
FHNS ZPS VLZBZL VFBCZ, ZPS RSAZ VBXZ LT KPHQP HA
ECUSXWXLECU.

Spanish Proverbs 8
EY OYQ LDBYCID WQ SA TLCDF, FYL VMDO SCOD CG YUE,
AYZLG VCUU PD ODV.

Swedish Proverbs 1
VTGYBN ERJ MV G NRASHB ERJ; VTGYBN VRYYRU MV TGHK
G VRYYRU.

Swedish Proverbs 2
LUEM DUQQ, AOWU POMU; UEC DUQQ, NAUI POMU; IAGYU DUQQ, BMUECAU POMU; CEDX DUQQ, QES POMU; AECU DUQQ, DOFU POMU; EYV EDD KOOV CAGYKQ EMU SOZMQ.

Swedish Proverbs 3
GYD'C CJQYE KEKM CJF YHG ZOTNFC ODCVH MYO NDYE EJFCJFQ CJF DFE YDF JYHGB EKCFQ.

Swedish Proverbs 4
EZV'J BCJ PZUM QZMMZA IZYC XORXCM JXGV PZUM FVCCQ.

Swedish Proverbs 5
PX P YRM R LDTS XDL SUSLN IPZS P IYDJFYI DX NDJ, P'M WS VPKEPQF LDTST XDL R GPXSIPZS.

Swedish Proverbs 6
FO EUYFOV OC COI MHFOSE CW MHI EOCK MHLM WINN NLEM RILY.

Swedish Proverbs 7

IMQ NPIHCV EI OMJOKQV KI W TFOQMV OM EIIV TIFKHMQ,
WMV HMOMJOKQV OM GONTIFKHMQ.

Swedish Proverbs 8

QPT SKNZA TY XPZ QWNZA WYG OWBZA PKA SKNKYC
ERTO XPZ QKYG? W EKAPZROWY.

Knowledge and Success 1

LMY DYLHYTPP WP W AWXELA NWA VT AL PCEGXTY XQWA
LMY DYLHYTPP EA TJMNWXELA. XQT QMFWA FEAJ EP LMY
GMAJWFTAXWZ YTPLMYNT.   —ULQA G. OTAATJR

Knowledge and Success 2

CLZ CZKC RXE CLZ TKZ YM BRX'K ZETGRCVYX VK CLRC LZ
MVXEK FSZRKTWZ VX CLZ ZDZWGVKZ YM LVK BVXE.
                              —PRGATZK BRWCVX URWJTX

Knowledge and Success 3

ZWGQG VY JP YDXW ZWVJO MY MJ DJTGQGYZVFMZG PU
MAGQMOG VJZGRRVOGJXG.   —WGJQI MTMFY

Knowledge and Success 4

KYFIXYC E OWVIH LYPCYY WV FKIYOOFPYKNY KWC
FQEPFKEIFWK KWC GWIX IWPYIXYC PW IW IXY QEMFKP
WV PYKFZD. OWRY, OWRY, OWRY, IXEI FD IXY DWZO WV
PYKFZD.   —TWOVPEKP EQELYZD QWUECI

Knowledge and Success 5
VR VF RJW NSPC UB SO WZXISRWZ NVOZ RU TW STDW RU
WORWPRSVO S RJUXYJR QVRJUXR SIIWLRVOY VR.
—SPVFRURDW

Power of Education 1
HBITVACDP CS AXH VWCMCAR AD MCSAHP AD VMFDSA
VPRAXCPL UCAXDIA MDSCPL RDIK AHFZHK DK RDIK SHMJ-
TDPJCBHPTH. —KDWHKA JKDSA

The Power of Education 2
QBUAGOEPS EH NZGO HUCVEVQH NZQS NZGO ZGH YQQS
KQGCSQB ZGH YQQS FPCWPOOQS. —Y. F. HIESSQC

The Power of Education 3
NPL OKFRNGCF CO LMKRDNGCF GJ NC PLZX WCK OACE
RPGZMPCCM FCN NC GEGNDNL DFWQCMW, QKN QL
WCKAJLZO DZZ NPL NGEL.

—BGMMK IAGJPFDEKANG

The Power of Education 4

KPVSV BSV KLI KOYVD IM VJCTBKFIA . . . IAV DPICZJ KVBTP
CD PIL KI RBNV B ZFWFAG, BAJ KPV IKPVS PIL KI ZFWV.

—QIPA BJBRD

The Power of Education 5

YJUOMGLFK LA VCYK WFU NYMJ GCY HLKY TNLKG.
YETYNLYKOY LA VCMG WFU ZYG LH WFU JFK'G.

—TYGY AYYZYN

Intelligent Thought 1

YI T QTR BKCW WKSCRVYNA, OC QTDD YR YNWRYNQR;
YI OC BK RVC WTSC RVYNA, IKJ RVC WTSC JCTWKN, OC
QTDD YR YNRCDDYACNQC. —OYDD QHLLX

Intelligent Thought 2

GVK GKTG LE S EXBTG-BSGK XMGKYYXUKMRK XT GVK
SHXYXGF GL VLYA GIL LJJLTKA XAKST XM WXMA SG
GVK TSWK GXWK SMA TGXYY BKGSXM GVK SHXYXGF GL
ENMRGXLM. —E. TRLGG EXGPUKBSYA

32

Intelligent Thought 3

KI VCZ CK T BCE ZSRSRMSZ, JOSZS TK EIJ IES FIZX TE JOS DIKGSNK TE GZCTKS IV TEJSNNTDSEBS.

—MSZJZCEX ZLKKSNN

Intelligent Thought 4

F NIQ INZB ULO WZZ QDO TRWFNL QDWQ F DWVO, TUQ WZZ QDWQ F MWN TIRRIP.

—PIISRIP PFZLIN

Intelligent Thought 5

TSNIUWNIT W UZWPJ UZI TVDITU TWAP UZHU WPUIBBWAIPU BWCI ILWTUT IBTIEZIDI WP UZI VPWYIDTI WT UZHU PSPI SC WU ZHT UDWIF US MSPUHMU VT.

—KWBB EHUUIDTSP

Knowledge and Wisdom 1

YH WTORZTX LQNLKX, EZO UAZNQHDCH NRQQ AZB LWSTROH KZT; KZT JTXB LWSTROH RB.

—XTDRH YLWU

33

Knowledge and Wisdom 2

HO UW MOYLMVOQL HIFH JOQ FKW VBYOKFYH VL F BKWFH
LHWC HO AYOPDWRBW.   —UWYTFXVY RVLKFWDV

Knowledge and Wisdom 3

FVAF RJ BVAF PSAXZRZM RJ. HOE JELLSZPH EZLSXJFAZL
JOISFVRZM HOE'KS EZLSXJFOOL APP HOEX PRCS, TEF RZ
A ZSB BAH.   —LOXRJ PSJJRZM

Knowledge and Wisdom 4

GXTCTUTV MQO LVT LRNTP SE MQO HLC PQ L ZQI, ATFF 'TK,
"HTVALSCFM S HLC!" AXTC YTA IORM LCP ESCP QOA XQG
AQ PQ SA.   —AXTQPQVT VQQRTUTFA

Knowledge and Wisdom 5

SMB CBXLTTLTX RG FTRHABOXB LD SMB OLDURIBWQ RG
DRPBSMLTX HB OR TRS ZTOBWDSNTO.

          —GWNTF MBWCBWS

34

Leaders and Followers 1

ZNBINLAFPJ AFTVZI XN XTLM TVO TH OFN VMINLAOBMIPMU
TH OFN MNNIA TH OFTAN QFT QTVZI XN BHHNRONI XW PO.
—GBLPBM BMINLATM

Leaders and Followers 2

RFTIFVACNH: OCF TVO SW LFOONGL ASEFSGF FRAF OS IS
ASEFOCNGL XSB JTGO ISGF KFZTBAF CF JTGOA OS IS NO.
—IJNLCO I. ΓNAΓGCSJFV

Leaders and Followers 3

PMJQD JV QDB MXJFJQK IP M FBMΛBT JH IP HFJRDQ
HBTWJOB UVFBHH JQ XB UVJQBA YJQD PMJQD JV DJH
LUHQJOB. —RBITRB RIBQDMFH

Leaders and Followers 4

EDY GYI EA WYMQT B TAAR KBQBTYC MZ GYYUMQT EDY
UYAUSY FDA DBEY KY BFBI JCAK EDAZY FDA BCY ZEMSS
NQRYXMRYR. —XBZYI ZEYQTYS

35

Leaders and Followers 5

CDHEDIRVQK QR ODFFQPO KDZKCD FZ UZIX MZI GZT UVDP
FVDG HID PZF ZYCQOHFDE.   —MIDE RJQFV

Close to Perfection 1

KJIYBYXO WLI MRAMEEMXAM FLJYBPJMK ZLQ; KJIYBYXO
WLI CMIWMAJYLX YK HMFLIPEYDYXO. —VPIIYMJ NIPYUMI

Close to Perfection 2

PFEHKUD YTKVB KEF DFPFBBKEL YNE HJF VJNTF. UH VNSTW
BFFR BHEKDQF UY NTW YEUFDWB TKPXFW PFEHKUD
ISUEXB.   —QNFHJF

Close to Perfection 3

WGQ VEORQRW WO BQTDQVWJOM Z BQTROM QYQT VOLQR
JR SGQM GQ DJEER OAW Z POI ZBBEJVZWJOM DOTL.

                                             —RWZMEQK P. TZMUZEE

Close to Perfection 4

ZVVFJS QCPJ JLXHS SC UZRF Z DFT ULVSZRFV. LD EFCEBF
OZY'S ZOOFES QCPJ LUEFJDFOSLCYV, SHZS'V SHFLJ
DZPBS. —GJ. GZILG U. WPJYV

Close to Perfection 5

NTOCDOD EBQ DJJY XJTGJSOCQW CW JLJTVOBCWA NTJ
OBQDJ EBQ SNWWQO NOONCW CO CW NWVOBCWA.
—JUAJWJ MJKNSTQCF

Complete Success 1

IBYYTII HI RAZ ZQT UTW ZA QXLLHRTII. QXLLHRTII HI ZQT
UTW ZA IBYYTII. HF WAB NAMT SQXZ WAB XDT OAHRE,
WAB SHNN GT IBYYTIIFBN. —XNGTDZ IYQSTHZKTD

Complete Success 2

HSVVIHH KH YIGMCKXI. KC KH TFMC TI VML ZMBI PU CFI
ZIHH TI FMXI ZMEI PU CFKLAH. —C. H. IGKPC

Complete Success 3

PKTTXPP ZP GEI A DXPIZGAIZEG IFAI HEK XYXQ QXATF. PKTTXPP ZP IFX VKAWZIH ES HEKQ UEKQGXH.

—UXGGZSXQ UABXP

Complete Success 4

WDRRFWW CW JU ZF TFNWDQFK EUJ WU TDRY ZP JYF IUWCJCUE JYNJ UEF YNW QFNRYFK CE VCBF NW ZP JYF UZWJNRVFW OYCRY YF YNW UGFQRUTF OYCVF JQPCEA JU WDRRFFK. —ZUUSFQ J. ONWYCEAJUE

Complete Success 5

SPETYP FGS ILEEPII: IMLDB NUTOP GMUPSI QSP IOPPYTCW; NGSV NUTOP GMUPSI QSP OGQFTCW; YSPYQSP NUTOP GMUPSI QSP YOQBTCW; QCD DSPQK NUTOP GMUPSI QSP NTIUTCW. —NTOOTQK Q. NQSD

Teachers and Students 1

WNB WYTB WBXFNBY ABHHBEAZ NKZ GTGKQZ XIXKEZW NKZ LOE GBYZLEXQ KEHQTBEFB.

—XCLZ DYLEZLE XQFLWW

Teachers and Students 2

TVS LSFXKOYS TSBOVSY TSEEN. TVS HKKF TSBOVSY
SUJEBXCN. TVS NZJSYXKY TSBOVSY FSLKCNTYBTSN. TVS
HYSBT TSBOVSY XCNJXYSN.　　　—RXEEXBL BYTVZY RBYF

Teachers and Students 3

DMMY UGFWPOSD OV MSG-LMHIUP KIGKFIFUOMS FSY
UPIGG-LMHIUPV UPGFUGI.　　　　—DFOA DMYQOS

Teachers and Students 4

EY YEK GDP JKM FQZZJ NKDZALKR MGK IKDZMG YF
PJXVDMGJ, TAEREKPP, DER BKEKNYPAMJ GARRKE ΛE
MGK PYQZ YF D HGAZR. MGK KFFYNM YF KUKNJ MNQK
KRQHDMAYE PGYQZR CK MY QEZYHT MGDM MNKDPQNK.
　　　　　　　　　　　　　　　—KXXD BYZRXDE

Teachers and Students 5

MCT JCOZT QHM OU MTQVCYXB YG OXZR MCT QHM OU
QJQLTXYYXB MCT XQMEHQZ VEHYOGYMR OU ROEXB FYXIG
UOH MCT WEHWOGT OU GQMYGURYXB YM QUMTHJQHIG.
　　　　　　　　　　　—QXQMOZT UHQXVT

At Work 1

JP IHF GH DH CHOM HZ IHFO GHQLX, IHFO GHQLX CJLL GH DH CHOM HZ IHF. JP IHF GH DH CHOM HZ IHFO NLQZ, IHFO NLQZ CJLL GH DH CHOM HZ IHF. CTQDBYBO GHHW DTJZGX CB RFJLW BZW FN RFJLWJZG FX.　　　　　—EJA OHTZ

At Work 2

KBKT PX QZ XPRSZ INU GN SUHHKKG, INU SZPOO VQBK ZN JNRA VQRG ZN SZQI ZVKRK.　　　　—RPHVQRG H. FPOOKR

At Work 3

DZHGH YGH TF KHJGHDK DF KNJJHKK. LD LK DZH GHKNOD FM VGHVYGYDLFT, ZYGA CFGP, OHYGTLTW MGFQ MYLONGH.　　　　　　　　—WHTHGYO JFOLT VFCHOO

At Work 4

UBHZXZTY CKH UIGGJUU AZBOKIB OQHF AKHM ZU SZMJ BHNZTY BK OQHXJUB AOJHJ NKI OQXJT'B LSQTBJF.

　　　　　　　　　　　　　　　—FQXZF PSN

At Work 5

IWQ TB DWFIJUW QKFQ QKW EDJCJIWXW QH MHDZ JB F
XJSQ, QKFQ EHMWD QH MHDZ JB F AIWBBJGX, QKFQ IHCW
HS MHDZ JB BTYYWBB.   —VFCJV H. PYZFN

Chocolate and Roses 1
YUU F JZYUUE XZZD FS UMGZ, COA Y UFAAUZ TRMTMUYAZ
XMK YXD ARZX DMZSX'A ROJA!   —TRYJUZS STROUN

Chocolate and Roses 2
AUG JGW JOMG IUNMEGJM OL EPMMNOY,
PYW AUG IUNAG JOMG TJGPAUGM OL ZOHG;
O, AUG JGW JOMG NM P LPZBOY,
PYW AUG IUNAG JOMG NM P WOHG.

                              —KOUY TOSZG O'JGNZZS

Chocolate and Roses 3
SR'F UZR REAR PEZPZHARYF ACY A FLBFRSRLRY DZC HZWY.
HZWY SF A FLBFRSRLRY DZC PEZPZHARY. PEZPZHARY SF,
HYR'F DAPY SR, DAC VZCY CYHSABHY REAU A VAU.

                              —VSCAUMA SUOCAV

Chocolate and Roses 4
MTE K PKII AMZV UWVV CVEB NF JNBVB
MTE M UWNDBMTE FJMHJMTU XNBKVB.

                              —OWJKBUNXWVJ AMJINPV

44

Chocolate and Roses 5

LUXH EHUETH KWH KTRKPL FWAXDTOJF DHBKALH WULHL
SKIH QSUWJL. O KX QSKJMVAT QSKQ QSUWJL SKIH
WULHL. —KTESUJLH MKWW

Out on a Date 1

UJ YKUATZSF RCZWVE HTFSCT YCUS TA LWZP C ASFMSYZ
ESVZGSUCV. XZWGG, W'NS EKZ CVKZPSF ZPFSS EKSX.
—XCGGJ AKAGWV

Out on a Date 2

LVKGLZ BRGVI KA? UBFWZIB NFGUTMBLI, CBK BSQALZGS,
BSQ KBII QBKGS. IMBI'Z JMG W'K QBIWSH.
—RAS BNNFAUT

Out on a Date 3

JC YZTWNJGIBLZ'Q WSWLIC. QBL'Q NTISWY. BL'Q TOGXI
WSWLIC-IBZLL. SI'Q YGSWY YZLTI. IBLC WLRLZ TZYXL. IBLC
FTW'I BLTZ LTFB GIBLZ.

—FTIBLZSWL ETNJTW

Out on a Date 4

Z KVTM QWYMQ W JZPI KV YFM YPWTX YMWR. ZY QZQV'Y
UKPX KLY. GFM XMAY JZBZVJ RM YFM PLVWPKLVQ.

—GTKYY PKMOMV

Out on a Date 5

IHFTOXIIU HWCI BMI AIUB NWBIU. XOG NOY'B MWQI BO FRVC
BMIH GF WYN BMIX'DI WTZWXU BWK-NINGVBRATI.

—WYNX ZWDMOT

Friendship 1

N ZTSDFK SL EFD HYE CDQSDADL SF WEP HYDF WEP YNAD
JDNLDK GE CDQSDAD SF WEPTLDQZ.   —KEFFN TECDTGL

Friendship 2

DZNXTIN SDZ LNHKDBYFVM UFBY BYM LPQQMWFZAL TQ
D QWFMZI, XPB FB WMEPFWML D RMWN QFZM ZDBPWM
BT LNHKDBYFVM UFBY D QWFMZI'L LPSSMLL.

—TLSDW UFJIM

Friendship 3

V UFXXCM UCXUJXMKFMJ FGG WB LKVJXZRAVO CX
FXB RVXDGJ CXJ CL WB LKVJXZR HJUFNRJ XC CXJ VR
UCWOGJMJ JXCNDA VX AVWRJGL.   —FXFVR XVX

Friendship 4

YZE UDENYEAY AJEEYEQED LF ZHTNQ RSFE SA FDSEQWAZSC.
YL DNSAE YZSA YL YZE ZSUZEAY CSYKZ LF EQBLMTEQY, SA
N AEKDEY JZSKZ OHY FEJ WSAKLVED.

                                —BLACCZ NWWSALQ

Friendship 5

UCAQSLITAD XAJT KSQIQWU AI OWW-AFDKCJOSJ EQROPIQ
XAJTKPJ AJ KSQ ROSSKJ EQ UCAQSLI XAJT OSBKSQ QWIQ
AS JTQ XKCWL.   —QWQOSKC CKKIQNQWJ

Hugs and Kisses 1

S AVLL VL S MHJNMZ COVFA XNLVEDNX GZ DSCPON CH
LCHI LINNFY TYND THOXL GNFHBN LPINOUMPHPL.

                                —VDEOVX GNOEBSD

Hugs and Kisses 2

MK MV KNA QFVVMZC KNFK MV MC F TMVV KNFK HMIAV KZ MK MKV VOAAKCAVV; MK MV KNA FWWAPKMZC MC F TMVV KNFK VFCPKMWMAV MK. —PNYMVKMFC CAVKALL DZIAA

Hugs and Kisses 3

UD GLZ NEH HQHE UR BLZAC NM CL FPHCPHE LE RLC GLZ MPLZOB IUMM N WEHCCG SUEO, NOFNGM SUQH PHE CPH AHRHDUC LD N BLZAC. —CPLJNM XNEOGOH

Hugs and Kisses 4

HKA JCVIZ CP F QDJJ DJ ICH JC UCVZ FJ HKFH CP F TFIICI, WVH DHJ ATKC UFJHJ F RXAFH ZAFU UCIRAX. —CUDEAX MAIZAUU KCUGAJ

Hugs and Kisses 5

FXKKXEO HRB ELP KQCTRY OTCHK, DSP PWTB ATCPRXEGB GLUTC CTKXKPREAT. —GLSXKT TCXAFKLE

The Power of Love 1

QTS VJSG IJO KPJOSDO YJZ MPJR NJFS HZO NJFS OJ GJRS SCOSIO KPJOSDOG YJZ MPJR QTS. —XSQIIS RJPSQZ

The Power of Love 2

JWFIF OE ULSC ULF WHGGOLFEE OL SONF, JU SUZF HLY XF
SUZFY. —RFUIRF EHLY

The Power of Love 3

YKJL GRC FRBJ MRZJRLJ, UFF GRCE MUBJS-CN YIMKJM
MVUEV DRZILT RCV. —JFIWUHJVK HRYJL

The Power of Love 4

P ARCX IRO NRY RNAI MRU HQEY IRO EUX, QOY MRU HQEY
P ES HQXN P ES HPYQ IRO.

—XAPVEGXYQ GEUUXYY GURHNPNW

The Power of Love 5

OMF, JME LXX, XDPT WDJ H VMRX JME AMFX, YMWDJ
AMFX YTDC JXLYXFWDJ DCW VXLL YTDC YMAMFFMB.

—FMLXAMCWX IXFDFW

Getting Hitched 1

C HCQQY VCWWOCAK ON C BPFA XPFUKWNCDOPF THOXH
CBTCYN NKKVN DPP NHPWD. —CFEWK VCZWPON

49

Getting Hitched 2

GIMCM AY TQ UQCM FQVMFB, DCAMTPFB, ETP LIECUATZ CMFEGAQTYIAS, LQUUWTAQT, QC LQUSETB GIET E ZQQP UECCAEZM. —UECGAT FWGIMC

Getting Hitched 3

ACV LKIV NKS XPGVEA XP Q LQIIXQZV, ACV LKIV GQJSQFJV XA FVWKLVE. —QLN ZIQPA

Getting Hitched 4

N GHFWK CNXXVNAY VG WHE RNGYK HW MHCDSYEY BXNWIWYGG; VE VG RNGYK HW N GYWGVRSY XYEVMYWMY. —CHXXVG S. YXWGE

Getting Hitched 5

MZ NYS DILLMIVJ IN YOJN XFJZSMYN, AUJN MS MZ IGGJVJE, HLYD SUJ WJVMNNMNV YH SUJ AYLGE, SUIS ZFTU IZ ILJ MN SUJ MNZSMSFSMYN AMZU SY VJS YFS, INE ZFTU IZ ILJ YFS AMZU SY VJS MN? —LIGOU AIGEY JDJLZYN

Hints

Homer 1 G=E	American Proverbs 2 R=D
Homer 2 L=F	American Proverbs 3 R=D
Edgar Allan Poe 1 W=B	American Proverbs 4 F=L
Edgar Allan Poe 2 F=D	American Proverbs 5 S=C
Shakespeare 1 E=I	American Proverbs 6 N=F
Shakespeare 2 D=G	American Proverbs 7 M=L
Henry David Thoreau 1 P=A	American Proverbs 8 W=R
Henry David Thoreau 2 T=F	Chinese Proverbs 1 K=M
J. R. R. Tolkien 1 A=O	Chinese Proverbs 2 K=H
J. R. R. Tolkien 2 R=E	Chinese Proverbs 3 T=N
Mark Twain 1 S=P	Chinese Proverbs 4 Q=Y
Mark Twain 2 K=W	Chinese Proverbs 5 Z=D
Other Authors 1 D=P	Chinese Proverbs 6 P=R
Other Authors 2 O=W	Chinese Proverbs 7 E=G
Other Authors 3 Q=P	Chinese Proverbs 8 Z=S
Other Authors 4 X=L	English Proverbs 1 O=T
Other Authors 5 J=N	English Proverbs 2 I=B
Other Authors 6 I=S	English Proverbs 3 F=G
Other Authors 7 H=T	English Proverbs 4 T=L
Other Authors 8 C=M	English Proverbs 5 J=W
American Proverbs 1 C=G	English Proverbs 6 H=M

English Proverbs 7 F=K

English Proverbs 8 D=R

French Proverbs 1 I=N

French Proverbs 2 L=W

French Proverbs 3 C=L

French Proverbs 4 N=C

French Proverbs 5 C=G

French Proverbs 6 Z=H

French Proverbs 7 E=R

French Proverbs 8 Y=M

Italian Proverbs 1 D=L

Italian Proverbs 2 B=D

Italian Proverbs 3 C=S

Italian Proverbs 4 H=S

Italian Proverbs 5 H=T

Italian Proverbs 6 N=F

Italian Proverbs 7 Q=L

Italian Proverbs 8 Y=B

Japanese Proverbs 1 Y=D

Japanese Proverbs 2 Q=V

Japanese Proverbs 3 T=G

Japanese Proverbs 4 U=R

Japanese Proverbs 5 B=C

Japanese Proverbs 6 X=P

Japanese Proverbs 7 E=H

Japanese Proverbs 8 V=N

Native American Proverbs 1 T=L

Native American Proverbs 2 P=W

Native American Proverbs 3 G=M

Native American Proverbs 4 M=P

Native American Proverbs 5 P=W

Native American Proverbs 6 R=K

Native American Proverbs 7 Y=B

Native American Proverbs 8 J=M

Spanish Proverbs 1 Z=D

Spanish Proverbs 2 E=W

Spanish Proverbs 3 C=I

Spanish Proverbs 4 I=U

Spanish Proverbs 5 F=M

Spanish Proverbs 6 D=P

Spanish Proverbs 7 V=P

Spanish Proverbs 8 A=Y

Swedish Proverbs 1 E=J

Swedish Proverbs 2 D=L

Swedish Proverbs 3 E=W

Swedish Proverbs 4 M=R

Swedish Proverbs 5 T=S

Swedish Proverbs 6 E=S

Swedish Proverbs 7 T=F

Swedish Proverbs 8 Q=W

Knowledge and Success 1 G=F

Knowledge and Success 2 A=Q

Knowledge and Success 3 P=G

Knowledge and Success 4 S=A

The Power of Education 1 J=F

The Power of Education 2 I=K

The Power of Education 3 B=J

The Power of Education 4 J=D

The Power of Education 5 Z=G

Intelligent Thought 1 L=P

Intelligent Thought 2 R=C

Intelligent Thought 3 E=N

Intelligent Thought 4 P=W

Intelligent Thought 5 S=O

Knowledge and Wisdom 1 Y=B

Knowledge and Wisdom 2 U=B

Knowledge and Wisdom 3 M=G

Knowledge and Wisdom 4 U=V

Knowledge and Wisdom 5 M=H

Leaders and Followers 1 G=M

Leaders and Followers 2 I=D

Leaders and Followers 3 R=G

Leaders and Followers 4 X=C

Leaders and Followers 5 M=F

Close to Perfection 1 N=B

Close to Perfection 2 H=T

Close to Perfection 3 T=R

Close to Perfection 4 G=D

Close to Perfection 5 F=X

Complete Success 1 S=W

Complete Success 2 G=L

Complete Success 3 U=J

Complete Success 4 Y=H

Complete Success 5 N=W

Teachers and Students 1 X=A

Teachers and Students 2 R=W

Teachers and Students 3 D=G

Teachers and Students 4 X=M

Teachers and Students 5 H=R

At Work 1 A=M

At Work 2 O=L

At Work 3 W=G

At Work 4 P=B

At Work 5 Z=K

Chocolate and Roses 1 U=L

Chocolate and Roses 2 T=B

Chocolate and Roses 3 V=M

Chocolate and Roses 4 O=C

Chocolate and Roses 5 M=K

Out on a Date 1 A=P

Out on a Date 2 N=F

Out on a Date 3 W=N

Out on a Date 4 O=B

Out on a Date 5 Z=W

Friendship 1 K=D

Friendship 2 U=W

Friendship 3 X=N

Friendship 4 B=J

Friendship 5 D=P

Hugs and Kisses 1 E=G

Hugs and Kisses 2 I=V

Hugs and Kisses 3 X=C

Hugs and Kisses 4 M=W

Hugs and Kisses 5 F=K

The Power of Love 1 X=J

The Power of Love 2 R=G

The Power of Love 3 H=B

The Power of Love 4 G=B

The Power of Love 5 L=S

Getting Hitched 1 W=R

Getting Hitched 2 L=C

Getting Hitched 3 G=V

Getting Hitched 4 S=L

Getting Hitched 5 D=M

Answers

BOOKWORM CRYPTOGRAMS

Homer 1
I detest that man who hides one thing in the depths of his heart, and speaks for another.

Homer 2
It is equally offensive to speed a guest who would like to stay and to detain one who is anxious to leave.

Edgar Allan Poe 1
I would define, in brief, the Poetry of words as the Rhythmical Creation of Beauty. Its sole arbiter is Taste.

Edgar Allan Poe 2
Ah, distinctly I remember it was in the bleak December;
And each separate dying ember wrought its ghost upon the floor.

Shakespeare 1

Shall I compare thee to a summer's day? Thou art more lovely and more temperate: Rough winds do shake the darling buds of May, And summer's lease hath all too short a date.

Shakespeare 2

Be not afraid of greatness. Some are born great, some achieve greatness, and some have greatness thrust upon 'em.

Henry David Thoreau 1

The man who goes alone can start today, but he who travels with another must wait till that other is ready.

Henry David Thoreau 2

The most I can do for my friend is simply to be his friend. I have no wealth to bestow on him. If he knows that I am happy in loving him, he will want no other reward. Is not friendship divine in this?

J. R. R. Tolkien 1

I cordially dislike allegory in all its manifestations, and always have done since I grew old and wary enough to detect its presence.

J. R. R. Tolkien 2

A box without hinges, key, or lid, yet golden treasure inside is hid.

Mark Twain 1

Suppose you were an idiot . . . And suppose you were a member of Congress . . . But I repeat myself.

Mark Twain 2

The only way to keep your health is to eat what you don't want, drink what you don't like, and do what you'd rather not.

Other Authors 1

Men can only be happy when they do not assume that the object of life is happiness.   —George Orwell

Other Authors 2

What really knocks me out is a book that, when you're all done reading it, you wish the author that wrote it was a terrific friend of yours and you could call him up on the phone whenever you felt like it. —J. D. Salinger

Other Authors 3

Appreciation is a wonderful thing: It makes what is excellent in others belong to us as well. — Voltaire

Other Authors 4

I always like to know everything about my new friends, and nothing about my old ones. —Oscar Wilde

Other Authors 5

Never trust anything that can think for itself if you can't see where it keeps its brain. —J. K. Rowling

Other Authors 6

Where so many hours have been spent in convincing myself that I am right, is there not some reason to fear I may be wrong?

—Jane Austen

Other Authors 7

If you don't have the time to read, you don't have the time or the tools to write.   —Stephen King

Other Authors 8

Be who you are and say what you feel, because those who mind don't matter and those who matter don't mind.

—Dr. Seuss

WISDOM OF PROVERBS

American Proverbs 1

Age gives good advice when it is no longer able to give a bad example.

American Proverbs 2
For age and want save while you may, no morning sun lasts a whole day.

American Proverbs 3
A dose of adversity is often as needful as a dose of medicine.

American Proverbs 4
The more arguments you win, the fewer friends you will have.

American Proverbs 5
Like a fence, character cannot be strengthencd by whitewash.

American Proverbs 6
A benevolent man should allow a few faults in himself to keep his friends in countenance.

American Proverbs 7
It is bad luck to fall out of a thirteenth-story window on Friday.

American Proverbs 8

Keep your eyes wide open before marriage, half shut afterwards.

Chinese Proverbs 1

Give a man a fish and you feed him for a day. Teach a man to fish and you feed him for a lifetime.

Chinese Proverbs 2

He who asks is a fool for five minutes, but he who does not ask remains a fool forever.

Chinese Proverbs 3

When you have only two pennies left in the world, buy a loaf of bread with one, and a lily with the other.

Chinese Proverbs 4

You think you lost your horse? Who knows, he may bring a whole herd back to you someday.

Chinese Proverbs 5
A friend is someone who dances with you in the sunlight and walks beside you in the shadows.

Chinese Proverbs 6
When you are poor, neighbors close by will not come; once you become rich, you'll be surprised by visits from (alleged) relatives afar.

Chinese Proverbs 7
A good fortune may forbode a bad luck, which may in turn disguise a good fortune.

Chinese Proverbs 8
Happiness is like a sunbeam, which the least shadow intercepts, while adversity is often as the rain of spring.

English Proverbs 1
Don't count your chickens before they're hatched.

English Proverbs 2
A bird in the hand is worth two in the bush.

English Proverbs 3
The grass is always greener on the other side of the fence.

English Proverbs 4
A good surgeon has an eagle's eye, a lion's heart, and a lady's hand.

English Proverbs 5
Early to bed and early to rise makes a man healthy, wealthy, and wise.

English Proverbs 6
A man may lead a horse to water, but cannot make him drink.

English Proverbs 7
He that eats of the king's goose shall be choked with feathers.

English Proverbs 8
There is nothing which we receive with so much reluctance as advice.

French Proverbs 1
Fortune is a woman; if you neglect her today do not expect to regain her tomorrow.

French Proverbs 2
What! No star, and you are going out to sea? Marching, and you have no music? Traveling, and you have no book? What! No love, and you are going out to live?

French Proverbs 3
A lie travels round the world while truth is putting her boots on.

French Proverbs 4
The poor man commands respect; the beggar must always excite anger.

French Proverbs 5

Ingratitude is a kind of weakness; clever men are not ungrateful.

French Proverbs 6

If the doctor cures the sun sees it, but if he kills the earth hides it.

French Proverbs 7

It is only at the tree loaded with fruit that the people throw stones.

French Proverbs 8

Love is the dawn of marriage, and marriage is the sunset of love.

Italian Proverbs 1

Tell not all you know, believe not all you hear, do not all you are able.

Italian Proverbs 2

If the patient dies, the doctor has killed him, but if he gets well, the saints have saved him.

Italian Proverbs 3
Give neither counsel nor salt till you are asked for it.

Italian Proverbs 4
Between saying and doing many a pair of shoes is worn out.

Italian Proverbs 5
In buying a horse and taking a wife, shut your eyes and commend yourself to God.

Italian Proverbs 6
Fill your glass when it is empty, empty it when it is full, never leave it empty, never leave it full.

Italian Proverbs 7
A pitcher that goes to the well often is likely to get broken.

Italian Proverbs 8
There is no need to bind up one's head before it is broken.

Japanese Proverbs 1

If you stand up like a nail you will get hammered down.

Japanese Proverbs 2

Vision without action is daydream. Action without vision is nightmare.

Japanese Proverbs 3

A single arrow is easily broken, but not ten in a bundle.

Japanese Proverbs 4

Better to be a crystal and to be broken, than to be a tile upon the housetop.

Japanese Proverbs 5

Don't rejoice over him that goes, before you see him that comes.

Japanese Proverbs 6

If I peddle salt, it rains; if I peddle flour, the wind blows.

Japanese Proverbs 7

If you wish to learn the highest truths, begin with the alphabet.

Japanese Proverbs 8

Never trust a woman, even if she has borne you seven children.

Native American Proverbs 1

It is better to have less thunder in the mouth and more lightning in the hand.

Native American Proverbs 2

Treat the earth well. It was not given to you by your parents, it was loaned to you by your children.

Native American Proverbs 3

Do not judge your neighbor until you walk two moons in his moccasins.

Native American Proverbs 4

You can't wake a person who is pretending to be asleep.

Native American Proverbs 5

A people without history is like wind on the buffalo grass.

Native American Proverbs 6

Speak truth in humility to all people. Only then can you be a true man.

Native American Proverbs 7

Don't walk behind me; I may not lead. Don't walk in front of me; I may not follow. Walk beside me that we may be as one.

Native American Proverbs 8

A man can't get rich if he takes proper care of his family.

Spanish Proverbs 1

If you lean to a good tree you will be protected by a good shadow.

Spanish Proverbs 2

If your wife wants to throw you off the roof, try to find a low one.

Spanish Proverbs 3
Tell me who is by your side and I'll tell you who you are.

Spanish Proverbs 4
Don't speak unless you can improve upon the silence.

Spanish Proverbs 5
Love, pain, and money cannot be kept secret; they soon betray themselves.

Spanish Proverbs 6
An ounce of blood is worth more than a pound of friendship.

Spanish Proverbs 7
A man who prides himself on his ancestry is like the potato plant, the best part of which is underground.

Spanish Proverbs 8
Do not rejoice at my grief, for when mine is old, yours will be new.

Swedish Proverbs 1

Shared joy is a double joy; shared sorrow is half a sorrow.

Swedish Proverbs 2

Fear less, hope more; eat less, chew more; whine less, breathe more; talk less, say more; hate less, love more; and all good things are yours.

Swedish Proverbs 3

Don't throw away the old bucket until you know whether the new one holds water.

Swedish Proverbs 4

Don't let your sorrow come higher than your knees.

Swedish Proverbs 5

If I had a rose for every time I thought of you, I'd be picking roses for a lifetime.

Swedish Proverbs 6
In spring no one thinks of the snow that fell last year.

Swedish Proverbs 7
One should go invited to a friend in good fortune, and uninvited in misfortune.

Swedish Proverbs 8
Who lives on the waves and makes his living from the wind? A fisherman.

KNOWLEDGE AND SUCCESS

Knowledge and Success 1
Our progress as a nation can be no swifter than our progress in education. The human mind is our fundamental resource.
—John F. Kennedy

Knowledge and Success 2

The test and the use of man's education is that he finds pleasure in the exercise of his mind.   Jacques Martin Barzun

Knowledge and Success 3

There is no such thing as an underestimate of average intelligence.   —Henry Adams

Knowledge and Success 4

Neither a lofty degree of intelligence nor imagination nor both together go to the making of genius. Love, love, love, that is the soul of genius.   —Wolfgang Amadeus Mozart

Knowledge and Success 5

It is the mark of an educated mind to be able to entertain a thought without accepting it.   —Aristotle

Power of Education 1

Education is the ability to listen to almost anything without losing your temper or your self-confidence.   —Robert Frost

The Power of Education 2
Education is what survives when what has been learned has been forgotten. —B. F. Skinner

The Power of Education 3
The function of education is to help you from childhood not to imitate anybody, but be yourself all the time.

—Jiddu Krishnamurti

The Power of Education 4
There are two types of education . . . One should teach us how to make a living, and the other how to live. —John Adams

The Power of Education 5
Education is when you read the fine print. Experience is what you get if you don't. —Pete Seeger

Intelligent Thought 1
If a cat does something, we call it instinct; if we do the same thing, for the same reason, we call it intelligence.

—Will Cuppy

Intelligent Thought 2

The test of a first-rate intelligence is the ability to hold two opposed ideas in mind at the same time and still retain the ability to function. —F. Scott Fitzgerald

Intelligent Thought 3

So far as I can remember, there is not one word in the Gospels in praise of intelligence. —Bertrand Russell

Intelligent Thought 4

I not only use all the brains that I have, but all that I can borrow. —Woodrow Wilson

Intelligent Thought 5

Sometimes I think the surest sign that intelligent life exists elsewhere in the universe is that none of it has tried to contact us. —Bill Watterson

Knowledge and Wisdom 1

Be curious always, for knowledge will not acquire you; you must acquire it. —Sudie Back

Knowledge and Wisdom 2

To be conscious that you are ignorant is a great step to knowledge. —Benjamin Disraeli

Knowledge and Wisdom 3

That is what learning is. You suddenly understand something you've understood all your life, but in a new way.

—Doris Lessing

Knowledge and Wisdom 4

Whenever you are asked if you can do a job, tell 'em, "Certainly I can!" Then get busy and find out how to do it.

—Theodore Roosevelt

Knowledge and Wisdom 5

The beginning of knowledge is the discovery of something we do not understand. —Frank Herbert

Leaders and Followers 1
Leadership should be born out of the understanding of the needs of those who would be affected by it.

—Marian Anderson

Leaders and Followers 2
Leadership: the art of getting someone else to do something you want done because he wants to do it.

—Dwight D. Eisenhower

Leaders and Followers 3
Faith in the ability of a leader is of slight service unless it be united with faith in his justice.　　　—George Goethals

Leaders and Followers 4
The key to being a good manager is keeping the people who hate me away from those who are still undecided.

—Casey Stengel

Leaders and Followers 5

Leadership is getting people to work for you when they are not obligated. —Fred Smith

Close to Perfection 1

Striving for excellence motivates you; striving for perfection is demoralizing. —Harriet Braiker

Close to Perfection 2

Certain flaws are necessary for the whole. It would seem strange if old friends lacked certain quirks. —Goethe

Close to Perfection 3

The closest to perfection a person ever comes is when he fills out a job application form. —Stanley J. Randall

Close to Perfection 4

Assert your right to make a few mistakes. If people can't accept your imperfections, that's their fault.

—Dr. David M. Burns

Close to Perfection 5

Artists who seek perfection in everything are those who cannot attain it in anything.　　　　　　　　　　—Eugene Delacroix

Complete Success 1

Success is not the key to happiness. Happiness is the key to success. If you love what you are doing, you will be successful.
　　　　　　　　　　—Albert Schweitzer

Complete Success 2

Success is relative. It is what we can make of the mess we have made of things.　　　　　　　　　　—T. S. Eliot

Complete Success 3

Success is not a destination that you ever reach. Success is the quality of your journey.　　　　　　　　　　—Jennifer James

Complete Success 4

Success is to be measured not so much by the position that one has reached in life as by the obstacles which he has overcome while trying to succeed.　　　　　　　　　　—Booker T. Washington

Complete Success 5

Recipe for success: Study while others are sleeping; work while others are loafing; prepare while others are playing; and dream while others are wishing.   —William A. Ward

Teachers and Students 1

The true teacher defends his pupils against his own personal influence.   —Amos Bronson Alcott

Teachers and Students 2

The mediocre teacher tells. The good teacher explains. The superior teacher demonstrates. The great teacher inspires.
—William Arthur Ward

Teachers and Students 3

Good teaching is one-fourth preparation and three-fourths theater.   —Gail Godwin

Teachers and Students 4

No one has yet fully realized the wealth of sympathy, kindness, and generosity hidden in the soul of a child. The effort of every true education should be to unlock that treasure.

—Emma Goldman

Teachers and Students 5

The whole art of teaching is only the art of awakening the natural curiosity of young minds for the purpose of satisfying it afterwards. —Anatole France

At Work 1

If you go to work on your goals, your goals will go to work on you. If you go to work on your plan, your plan will go to work on you. Whatever good things we build end up building us. —Jim Rohn

At Work 2

Even if at first you do succeed, you still have to work hard to stay there. —Richard C. Miller

At Work 3

There are no secrets to success. It is the result of preparation, hard work, learning from failure. —General Colin Powell

At Work 4

Striving for success without hard work is like trying to harvest where you haven't planted. —David Bly

At Work 5

Let us realize that the privilege to work is a gift, that power to work is a blessing, that love of work is success.

—David O. McKay

LOVE & ROMANCE

Chocolate and Roses 1

All I really need is love, but a little chocolate now and then doesn't hurt! —Charles Schulz

Chocolate and Roses 2

The red rose whispers of passion,
And the white rose breathes of love;
O, the red rose is a falcon,
And the white rose is a dove. —John Boyle O'Reilly

Chocolate and Roses 3

It's not that chocolates are a substitute for love. Love is a substitute for chocolate. Chocolate is, let's face it, far more reliable than a man. —Miranda Ingram

Chocolate and Roses 4

And I will make thee beds of roses
And a thousand fragrant posies. —Christopher Marlowe

Chocolate and Roses 5

Some people are always grumbling because roses have thorns. I am thankful that thorns have roses. —Alphonse Karr

Out on a Date 1

My computer dating bureau came up with a perfect gentleman. Still, I've got another three goes.   —Sally Poplin

Out on a Date 2

Rumors about me? Calista Flockhart, Pam Anderson, and Matt Damon. That's who I'm dating.   —Ben Affleck

Out on a Date 3

My grandmother's ninety. She's dating. He's about ninety-three. It's going great. They never argue. They can't hear each other.
            —Catherine Ladman

Out on a Date 4

I once dated a girl on the track team. It didn't work out. She kept giving me the runaround.   —Scott Roeben

Out on a Date 5

Employees make the best dates. You don't have to pick them up and they're always tax-deductible.   —Andy Warhol

Friendship 1

A friend is one who believes in you when you have ceased to believe in yourself.
—Donna Roberts

Friendship 2

Anybody can sympathize with the sufferings of a friend, but it requires a very fine nature to sympathize with a friend's success.
—Oscar Wilde

Friendship 3

I cannot concentrate all my friendship on any single one of my friends because no one is complete enough in himself.
—Anais Nin

Friendship 4

The greatest sweetener of human life is Friendship. To raise this to the highest pitch of enjoyment, is a secret which but few discover.
—Joseph Addison

Friendship 5

Friendship with oneself is all-important because without it one cannot be friends with anyone else in the world.

—Eleanor Roosevelt

Hugs and Kisses 1

A kiss is a lovely trick designed by nature to stop speech when words become superfluous. —Ingrid Bergman

Hugs and Kisses 2

It is the passion that is in a kiss that gives to it its sweetness; it is the affection in a kiss that sanctifies it.

—Christian Nestell Bovee

Hugs and Kisses 3

If you are ever in doubt as to whether or not you should kiss a pretty girl, always give her the benefit of a doubt.

—Thomas Carlyle

Hugs and Kisses 4

The sound of a kiss is not so loud as that of a cannon, but its echo lasts a great deal longer. —Oliver Wendell Holmes

Hugs and Kisses 5

Kissing may not spread germs, but they certainly lower resistance. —Louise Erickson

The Power of Love 1

Age does not protect you from love but love to some extent protects you from age. —Jeanne Moreau

The Power of Love 2

There is only one happiness in life, to love and be loved. —George Sand

The Power of Love 3

When you love someone, all your saved-up wishes start coming out. —Elizabeth Bowen

The Power of Love 4

I love you not only for what you are, but for what I am when I am with you. —Elizabeth Barrett Browning

The Power of Love 5

For, you see, each day I love you more, today more than yesterday and less than tomorrow. —Rosemonde Gerard

Getting Hitched 1

A happy marriage is a long conversation which always seems too short. —Andre Maurois

Getting Hitched 2

There is no more lovely, friendly, and charming relationship, communion, or company than a good marriage.

—Martin Luther

Getting Hitched 3

The more you invest in a marriage, the more valuable it becomes. —Amy Grant

Getting Hitched 4

A sound marriage is not based on complete frankness; it is based on a sensible reticence. —Morris L. Ernst

Getting Hitched 5

Is not marriage an open question, when it is alleged, from the beginning of the world, that such as are in the institution wish to get out, and such as are out wish to get in?

—Ralph Waldo Emerson

BRAIN POPS!

Try all of these flavors for a complete brain workout!